Pianoworks

BOOK 2

Janet and Alan Bullard

MUSIC DEPARTMENT

OXFORD
UNIVERSITY PRESS

Great Clarendon Street, Oxford OX2 6DP, England
198 Madison Avenue, New York, NY 10016, USA

Oxford University Press is a department of the University of Oxford.
It furthers the University's aim of excellence in research, scholarship,
and education by publishing worldwide

Oxford is a registered trademark of Oxford University Press
in the UK and in certain other countries

3 5 7 9 10 8 6 4 2

ISBN 978–0–19–336007–5

Music and text origination by
Barnes Music Engraving Ltd., East Sussex.
Printed in Great Britain on acid-free paper by
Halstan & Co. Ltd., Amersham, Bucks.

All pieces are original compositions or arrangements by the authors unless otherwise stated.

The authors would like to thank all the teachers, pupils, and friends who
have tried out the contents of this series, for their helpful comments and
advice, and also the editorial team at Oxford University Press for their
consistent encouragement and help.

Preface

Congratulations on taking that next step in your piano playing with *Pianoworks 2*!

As you know if you've progressed through *Pianoworks 1*, this series is designed for anyone, of whatever age, who prefers a more adult approach to their learning. By working through this book you will build on the skills you've already developed, and be introduced, at a steady pace, to new techniques and styles. You will encounter all kinds of piano music, which can be played on a traditional upright or grand piano, or on a digital piano with weighted, touch-sensitive keys.

Pianoworks 2 is suitable for those with a little experience of playing the piano, as well as those with past experience who need some revision. Every new idea is defined and explained in a methodical way, and the information is presented in a logical order, allowing you to progress to each stage at your own pace. An index is provided for easy reference, which, together with that in *Pianoworks 1*, provides a useful summary of the technical terms and signs you are likely to come across. The book contains more than thirty pieces, including original piano pieces, old and new, as well as arrangements of classical works and traditional melodies. These have been carefully selected to cover a range of styles and mirror the development of keyboard music.

The accompanying CD includes each piece recorded as a solo, and for a few pieces there is a 'duet' accompaniment to play along with, starting with a two-bar introduction. You will also find exercises to help you play by ear, harmonize melodies, and develop your improvisation skills.

The book contains all the information you need to continue your studies at this stage. However, it is a good idea to work through it with an experienced piano teacher, who will be able to address any difficulties and work at a pace that suits you.

Regular practice—perhaps 20–30 minutes every day—is the best way to make progress; a longer practice every now and then will not allow you to absorb the information as efficiently, so try to set aside a little time each day instead.

Pianoworks Collection 2 contains thirty more pieces for you to play, including classical favourites, popular songs, show tunes, and easy contemporary pieces. The collection is designed to be used alongside this book, to widen your repertoire and experience, and to reinforce the skills learnt so far.

Good luck, and enjoy your piano playing!

JANET AND ALAN BULLARD

Contents

The piano and its music

The music in this book was written between the early 1600s and the present day, which means some of the pieces were composed before the piano came into common use in around 1750. Corelli's *Sarabande* (page 13), Graupner's *Bourrée* (page 15)—both pieces from the **Baroque** period of musical history—and the earlier *Nann's Maske* (page 53) would have most likely been played on a harpsichord or a clavichord.

Both these instruments have a keyboard similar to the modern piano (sometimes with the colours of the keys reversed), but the insides are rather different, and neither has a sustaining pedal. On the **harpsichord** (and its smaller relatives the **spinet** and **virginal**), pressing the keys causes the strings to be plucked by a quill or leather plectrum. This gives a powerful and clear sound, but the volume of the note cannot be varied by the amount of weight on the key. On the **clavichord**, the keys are simply pivoted so the other end of them hits the string with a metal tangent. The sound can be controlled very expressively by the fingers, but the overall volume is very quiet and only suitable for a small room. Performances of early music on a modern piano therefore need to respect the musical style of the era while also adapting to the new instrument—sudden dynamic contrasts and extensive use of the sustaining pedal are unlikely to be appropriate in most cases.

In 1713 the French harpsichordist and composer François Couperin wrote:

> The harpsichord is perfect as to its compass, and brilliant in itself, but as it is impossible to swell out or diminish the volume of its sound, I shall always feel grateful to any who, by the exercise of infinite art supported by fine taste, contrive to render this instrument capable of expression.

Little did he know that an instrument that could do this had just been invented by the Italian harpsichord-maker Cristofori. By replacing the plectrums of the harpsichord with small leather or felt hammers, activated by a lever mechanism controlled by the keys, it was possible to vary the power of the sound directly with the fingers. Thus the new instrument was capable of being played 'piano e forte' (quiet and loud), which was soon to be abbreviated to create the name 'pianoforte' (or 'fortepiano') and, today, simply 'piano'.

Composers of the mid eighteenth century—the generations of Haydn and Mozart—were among the first to take advantage of the piano's expressive powers; Mozart's *Andante in E flat* (page 59), Hässler's *Ecossaise* (page 41), and Czerny's *Study in G* (page 29)—all characteristic of the elegant style of the **Classical** period—show the different kinds of textures that could be produced on the piano.

The sustaining pedal also started to come into use during the Classical period, although it didn't really become integral to the piano style until the nineteenth century. This coincided with the development of the iron (as opposed to wooden) frame, which gave the piano tauter strings and a wider expressive range. Pieces of this so-called **Romantic** period, such as Spindler's *Song Without Words* (page 17), Tchaikovsky's *Old French Song* (page 49), and Burgmüller's dramatic *Ballade* (page 66), make full use of the piano's colourful tone qualities and the sonority that can be achieved with the sustaining pedal.

From the **twentieth century** onwards composers began to widen and develop the language of music while continuing to explore the full resources of the piano, and for many the use of the sustaining pedal became an essential part of the piano's sound-world, as in Skempton's delicately resonant *Arpeggio* (page 57).

Semiquavers

The **semiquaver** (or sixteenth-note) lasts half the length of a quaver (eighth-note).

Semiquavers are often grouped in fours and are joined by a **double beam**.

semiquaver   or   four semiquavers   or

- Clap or play the following rhythms, remembering that the crotchet pulse will subdivide into four semiquavers.

track 1

(count) 1 2 1 2 1 2 1 2

track 2

(count) 1 2 3 1 2 3

track 3

(count) 1 2 3 4 1 2 3 4

- Now try using these exercises as rhythmic building blocks, adding pitches to create a melody.
- Use the five-finger hand position initially, and play with hands separately or with hands together in octaves.
- An example, using the 2/4 rhythm, is played on   **track 4**

A crotchet beat can also be subdivided into one quaver and two semiquavers (and vice versa):

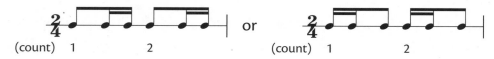

(count) 1 2   or   (count) 1 2

- Clap or play the following rhythm and then add pitches to make a melody as before.

track 5

(count) 1 2 3 4 1 2 3 4

In the lively *Scandinavian Dance* on the next page keep the semiquavers neat and even. As always, work on it with hands separately first; the left hand is in one hand position throughout (except for the final chord), but you will need to practise quick and accurate shifting between the positions in the right hand.

As well as a performance on the CD, there is also a duet part to play along with. As with all the duet parts in this book, there is a two-bar musical introduction before you start to play.

leggiero – lightly

🎵 **track 6** Solo
🎵 **track 7** Duet

Scandinavian Dance

Trad. Finnish

Scales and arpeggios, hands together

In Book 1 you learnt three scales and arpeggios: C major, G major, and F major. It's a good idea to make scale and arpeggio practice part of your regular piano routine, as much music is based on these patterns.

Later on you'll be introduced to more scales and arpeggios so that you get used to playing in different keys. For the moment we will revise the scales you already know, but this time playing with both hands together.

- Work on each hand separately first, and then put the hands together, playing slowly and steadily.
- Remember that the fingering for the right-hand F major scale is different from the fingering for C and G majors.

The *Two-Part Invention* on the next page makes use of these different keys. The title (often used by J. S. Bach) refers to the sense of musical conversation between the hands—the two 'parts' are independent from each other but share the same musical ideas. The music travels from C major to G major, back to C major, then to F major, and finally back to C major, making use of arpeggios and parts of the scales of each key. The transition from one key to another within a piece of music is called a **modulation**, and this can be seen and heard by the use of the accidentals of each new key. See if you can work out where the music modulates.

maestoso – majestically
poco – a little (**poco rit**. – slowing down a little)

track 8 Solo

Two-Part Invention

A. B. / J. B.

Minor keys

Every major key has a **relative minor** key that opens up a different sound-world; this is often more melancholy, mysterious, or even menacing in character.

To find the relative minor of any major key, count down a semitone and then a tone from the key note. Conversely, the **relative major** is a tone and a semitone higher than its relative minor.

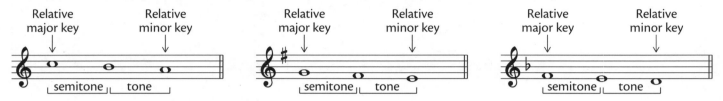

Originally from a medieval mystery play, the *Coventry Carol* is a lullaby in which Mary sings Jesus to sleep and laments Herod's resolve to kill all babes-in-arms. It is in the key of A minor, the relative minor of C major; thus, no key signature is used, but the accidentals (particularly G sharps) give the minor key its characteristic flavour. Accidentals are not normally written again when a note is tied, so the C sharp (and the A) are simply held on through the final three bars.

mesto – sorrowful

🔘 **track 9** Solo
🔘 **track 10** Duet

Coventry Carol

Trad. English

A minor scale and arpeggio

There are two main types of minor scales: harmonic and melodic. As we have seen, every minor key shares the key signature of its relative major, which is a tone plus a semitone higher.

In the **harmonic minor** scale the seventh note is raised by a semitone.

A minor scale (harmonic)

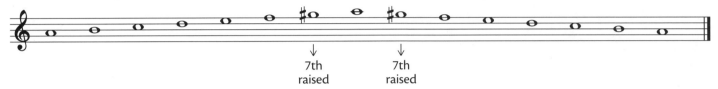

In the **melodic minor** scale the sixth and seventh notes are raised by a semitone on the way up, but not on the way down.

A minor scale (melodic)

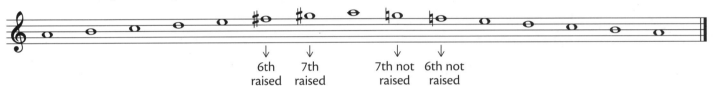

Minor arpeggios are shaped just like major arpeggios. There are no 'harmonic' and 'melodic' versions.

A minor arpeggio

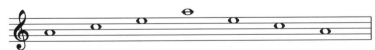

Melodies tend to use the smoother contours of the melodic minor scale, whereas the accompanying harmonies are frequently based on the slightly more jagged harmonic minor scale. In this book, we'll focus on playing the harmonic version of the scale.

- Practise the scale with hands separately first, and then with hands together.
- Be ready for the slightly wider stretch of the fingers between the sixth and seventh notes of the scale.

A minor scale (harmonic)

A minor arpeggio

E minor and D minor scales and arpeggios

These are the relative minors of G major and F major.

- Again, practise with hands separately first. The fingering patterns are the same as for A minor.

E minor (harmonic)

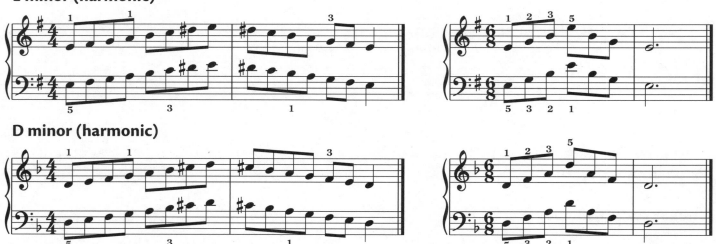

D minor (harmonic)

In *A Glimpse of Spain* the semiquaver decorations, the left-hand rhythm, and the minor key give the flavour of the habanera, a stately dance that originated in nineteenth-century Cuba but soon became popular in Spain. Keep the left hand steady and rhythmic, and imagine the dancers facing each other, gradually getting closer.

Again originating in Latin America and Spain, but in an earlier era, the *Sarabande* was a graceful dance that became popular in eighteenth-century Italy. With three beats in the bar, it is characterized by a rhythmic stress on the second beat—in this example mainly in the lower part—and should be played at an unhurried, steady tempo.

grazioso – gracefully

 **track 11** Solo

A Glimpse of Spain

J. B.

track **12** Solo

Sarabande

Arcangelo Corelli
(1653–1713)

Andante grazioso

New time signatures

2/2 or ¢   Here the bottom number tells us that we count in minims (half-notes), and the top number indicates that there are two beats in each bar.

🔘 **track 13**

3/2   Again, we count in minims, but this time there are three in each bar.

🔘 **track 14**

3/8   As with **6/8**, the bottom number tells us that we count in quavers (eighth-notes), but the top number indicates that there are only three in each bar.

🔘 **track 15**

Again, these rhythms can be made into melodies, as on page 6.

Pieces using these time signatures follow on the next three pages.

A note on fingering

In any piece of music the same fingering will not necessarily suit all players (hands come in all shapes and sizes!). We will continue to suggest fingering that will work for most people, but if any of it feels uncomfortable then you (or your teacher) can change it to something that works better.

In some piano music fingering isn't indicated at all, in which case it can be very helpful to pencil in your own fingering at important points, such as:

- hand position changes
- 'thumb under' passages
- places where the fingers move out of the five-finger position.

Consistent fingering will help you learn a piece securely and will result in a more reliable performance.

We do recommend that you use the scale and arpeggio fingering that we suggest.

The bourrée was a French dance popular in the eighteenth century. Although it has four crotchets per bar, it is easier to count in minims when the piece is played up to speed; thus the time signature is $\frac{2}{2}$, beginning on a crotchet upbeat.

Composers of the time frequently grouped sets of dances into **Suites** or **Partitas** to make a longer composition, and this movement comes from a keyboard partita by the prolific German composer Graupner, who was a contemporary of J. S. Bach and Handel—two of the most prominent composers of the **Baroque** period. Since this piece would originally have been played on the harpsichord, no dynamics were indicated by Graupner; we have made suggestions to adapt the piece for performance on the piano.

The second section of the movement is repeated. Notice that the repeat marks are at the end of the third beat of the bar, and thus the fourth beat is provided by the first note of the beginning of the repeated section. There should be no pause between the sections.

track 16 Solo

Bourrée

Christoph Graupner
(1683–1760)

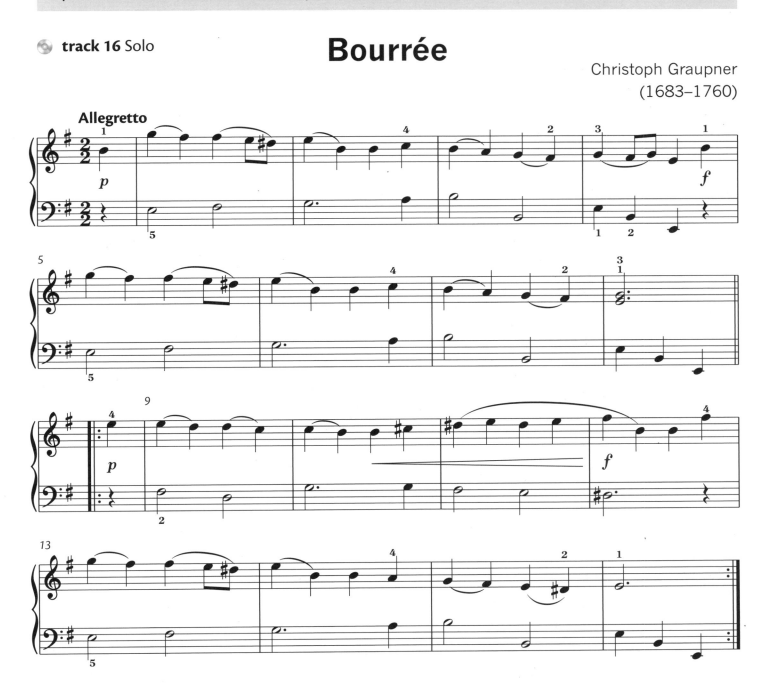

This is an excerpt from the well-known Hornpipe from Handel's 'Water Music', and the energetic rhythms of the opening bars contribute to the piece's lively character. Most of the time the hands move in the same rhythm, making it particularly important to keep a steady three-minims-in-a-bar pulse in your head.

Song Without Words, by the German pianist and composer Fritz Spindler, is again in 3-time, but here the beat is quavers. As the title suggests, the right hand should sing expressively while the left hand gives the lightest of support, aided by careful use of the pedal.

ritmico – rhythmically

 **track 17** Solo

Hornpipe

George Frideric Handel
(1685–1759)

track 18 Solo
track 19 Duet

Song Without Words

Fritz Spindler
(1817–1905)

Call and response exercises and improvisation

Book 1 included some call and response exercises on the CD. Listen to tracks 20–5 for more exercises and the opportunity to try some improvisation.

Dotted quavers

In Book 1 you learnt that a dot placed immediately after a note adds half the length of the note to it:

The same principle applies to the **dotted quaver**, which is equivalent to a quaver and a semiquaver tied together.

A dotted quaver is often followed by a semiquaver, and these are joined together by a beam—note the short second beam indicating the semiquaver.

• Try playing the following exercises to get used to this rhythm, keeping the pulse steady throughout.

track 26

track 27

The well-known theme from the slow movement of Dvořák's 'New World' Symphony presents a good opportunity to explore the dotted-quaver–semiquaver pattern. From 1892 to 1895 the Czech composer taught at a music college in New York, and he wrote this symphony while he was there. The section used in the arrangement on the next page is often said to show the influence of the American spirituals that he heard during his stay. Imagine the opening bars changing the scene—perhaps from Central Europe to the United States—and then play the melody with a soulful simplicity, keeping the tempo slow and steady.

misterioso – mysteriously
decresc. (**decrescendo**) – gradually getting quieter (the same as **diminuendo**)

Sometimes the sustaining pedal is notated without using horizontal brackets to indicate where it is pressed down and released. Instead, the following signs are used:

Ped. – press the sustaining pedal down   ✲ – raise the pedal

This is particularly useful when the pedal is held for a long time.

track 28 Solo

Theme from the 'New World' Symphony

Symphony No. 9, second movement

Antonín Dvořák
(1841–1904)

Triplets

A **triplet** is a group of three notes played in the time of two, indicated by a small 3 above or below the notes (sometimes with a bracket). The most common type of triplet is a group of three quavers, filling one crotchet beat, although the idea can also be applied to other note values.

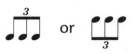

- Clap the following rhythms, keeping an even crotchet pulse throughout.
- Try counting '1-and 2-and' for ordinary quavers and '1-and-a 2-and-a' for triplet quavers.

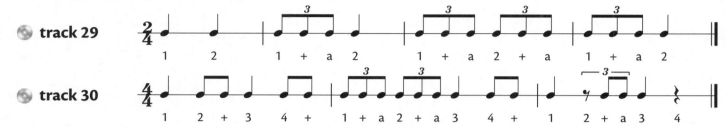

As before, you could turn these rhythm patterns into melodies.

> In *Lullaby* think of the right-hand melody as a song which is supported by a quiet and gentle accompaniment in the left hand. Aim to keep the triplets as even as possible, and take care not to confuse the triplet 3 with the fingering marks.

sostenuto – sustained

track 31 Solo

Lullaby

J. B.

Playing at sight

Being able to play a simple piece of music at first sight, with both hands together, is one of the most useful skills any pianist can have. Playing at sight (or sight-reading) requires a different approach from learning a new piece, but by working regularly at it you will find that the process of learning a new piece becomes quicker and easier.

Keeping the music moving forward, with a steady pulse and correct rhythm, is the primary aim for all sight-reading, so before playing the piece:

- check the time signature, count the pulse out loud, and then tap the rhythm with both hands at once
- check the starting note and the key signature, and get the fingers in position
- count yourself in.

Remember: even if you make a mistake, it's much more important to keep the music moving.

Here are three exercises to play at sight.

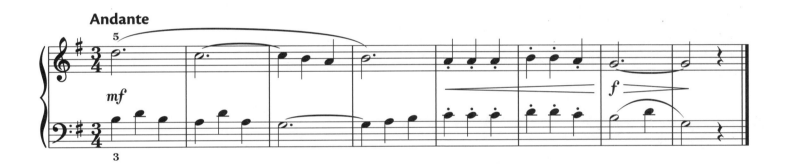

Two voices in one hand

In some piano music you'll find two different musical lines notated on a single stave, both of which are to be played with one hand. It can be helpful to think of these as two instruments or **parts** (often called **voices**), where the upper voice is notated with stems going up and the lower voice with stems going down.

- Practise these exercises, rotating the wrist slightly as the notes rise and fall.
- To avoid tension, relax the amount of weight on the tied notes once they have sounded, but make sure you keep them held down.

When both voices land on the same note, but each for a different length of time, the note is written twice to show the two separate durations. Thus in the following example the first D is notated as a crotchet for the top part and a minim for the lower part, but the note itself is played only once, by the fifth finger; as the second finger plays the G on the second beat, the fifth finger continues to hold the D down. Similarly the two stems on the G in bar 2 indicate that both voices share the note, although this time the duration is the same for each.

Mendelssohn: *Hark, the Herald Angels Sing*

When there are two voices on one stave, rests are placed higher or lower to clarify which part they belong to. This sometimes takes a little working out, but remember that the note durations in each of the two voices should normally add up to the complete length of the bar.

Amazing Grace

In *Floating on Air* on the next page aim for an expressive melodic line gently supported by a flowing **bass** line (lowest part). Listen carefully to ensure that each part is sustained as written.

non – not **troppo** – much (**adagio non troppo** – slow, but not too much)
allargando – broadening (slowing) the tempo
più – more (**più adagio** – slower)

track **32** Solo

Floating on Air

A. B.

New rhythms in compound time

As in simple time, music in compound time sometimes incorporates semiquavers.

- Practise clapping or tapping the following rhythm.

track 33

We will also meet the dotted-quaver–semiquaver rhythm in compound time.

- Clap or tap this rhythm, noting the difference in the position of the dots in bars 3 and 4.

track 34

Again, you could turn these rhythms into a melody to help fix them in your mind.

Greensleeves was a popular folk tune in Shakespeare's time and is mentioned in *The Merry Wives of Windsor*. As you'll see, the dotted-quaver–semiquaver pattern features strongly in the melodic line and gives the piece its characteristic lilting sound.

On the next page, *The Young Prince* uses many different rhythms within the ⁶⁄₈ pulse to achieve a feeling of graceful elegance. The piece is taken from the colourful orchestral suite *Sheherazade*, which is based on the Tales of the Arabian Nights.

Andantino – slightly faster than **Andante** **a, al** – to (**al fine** – to the end)

track 35 Solo
track 36 Duet

Greensleeves

Trad. English

track 37 Solo

The Young Prince

from *Sheherazade*

Nikolay Rimsky-Korsakov
(1844–1908)

Syncopation and swing

Syncopation

In Book 1 you came across the early jazz style, ragtime. This makes use of **syncopation**—an emphasis on beats other than the normal 'strong' beats. This can be achieved by adding rests on the strong beats, by tying notes across the beat, or by placing accents on the 'weaker' beats. Although syncopation is found in music of earlier centuries (used particularly to build up rhythmic excitement), it became a standard feature of much twentieth-century music.

This excerpt from a rag by Scott Joplin, one of the chief ragtime composers, is a good example of syncopation; each syncopated beat is marked with an S. You can hear it played on 🔘 **track 38**, with an accompaniment of steady crotchets in the left hand.

Scott Joplin: *The Easy Winners*

Swing

Jazz styles of the last 100 years or so have also made use of **swing** rhythm (or **swing quavers**).

Listen to the two short excerpts on 🔘 **tracks 39 and 40**

Both of these are notated in the same way: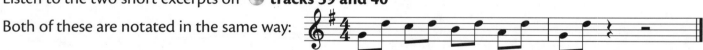

In the first excerpt, the quavers are played **straight** (this is jazz terminology for playing the quavers evenly, just as you have been doing so far).

In the second excerpt the same passage is **swung**, with the first quaver roughly twice as long as the second. Although it is possible to notate this rhythm as a crotchet and quaver grouped together with a triplet bracket, it is usually notated as ordinary quavers, with the word 'swing' included in the tempo marking.

When playing swing, jazz players will often give an extra push to the rhythm by slightly emphasizing the second quaver—another form of syncopation.

- Try clapping or playing the following rhythm, first of all straight (🔘 **track 41**) and then again using swing (🔘 **track 42**), repeating each several times.
- Remember that the crotchet pulse is unaffected.

If you like, you can also use the rhythm to make a melody.

Blue Cheese recollects the traditional blues style popular from the 1920s onwards: the left hand provides a steady pulse most of the way through, while the right hand plays swing quavers. Like *Travelling Blues* in Book 1, this piece uses the standard twelve-bar-blues chord sequence (twice), together with 'blue notes' G sharp and E flat.

rall. (rallentando) – gradually slowing down (same meaning as **ritardando**)

track **43** Solo
track **44** Duet

Blue Cheese

A. B.

Rolling along, swing quavers

Alberti bass

The **Alberti bass** (named after the Italian composer Alberti, who allegedly invented it) became a popular means of providing a left-hand accompaniment to a melody during the eighteenth century. It is created by breaking up a simple chord into separate notes, and playing those notes in a consistent pattern:

A good way to learn the note patterns of an Alberti bass is to practise with the notes simplified into their constituent chords.

- Try playing the first four bars of the *Study in G* on the next page with the Alberti bass changed into chords.

- When you have the shapes under your fingers, move on to playing the left-hand part as written, using the same fingering.
- Aim to make the quavers flow lightly. The movement should be predominantly from the fingers, though you may find it helpful to rotate the wrist very slightly when the stretch is wider.

The Alberti bass was popular during the **Classical** period, when the piano was superseding the harpsichord. Composers of the time, such as Haydn, Mozart, and Beethoven, frequently exploited the ability of the piano to achieve dynamic contrast according to the weight of the fingers on the keys. The Alberti bass provided an ideal opportunity for the pianist to project a flowing or decorative melody over a quieter, patterned accompaniment, and this 'melody with accompaniment' texture was to become typical of the late eighteenth and nineteenth centuries.

The Austrian composer Carl Czerny was a pupil of Beethoven and a teacher of Liszt. He wrote a wide range of music, but today he is best known for his educational works for the piano. The *Study in G* comes from his 'First Tutor' for the piano, Op. 599, which is a compendium of technical studies covering all the different textures and techniques of his time. '**Op.**' is short for '**Opus**' (Latin for 'work') and many composers number their output in this way, though few reach Op. 599!

Aim to play the melody with expression—perhaps imagine a violin or flute playing the right-hand part and 'balance' the sound so that the left hand is quieter. Try using the sustaining pedal for added colour, depressing it on the first quaver of each left-hand group and releasing it on the fourth.

track 45 Solo

Study in G

Op. 599 No. 4

Carl Czerny
(1791–1857)

Andante espressivo

Contrasts in touch between the hands

Contrasts in **touch** are an important aspect of playing the piano musically and expressively.

Staccato and legato

Often we need to use two kinds of **articulation** at the same time, for example legato in one hand and staccato in the other.

- Practise the following exercises to build up this technique.
- Start by playing just the first note in each hand, holding the legato note down while bouncing lightly off the staccato note, and then play each exercise in full, slowly at first.

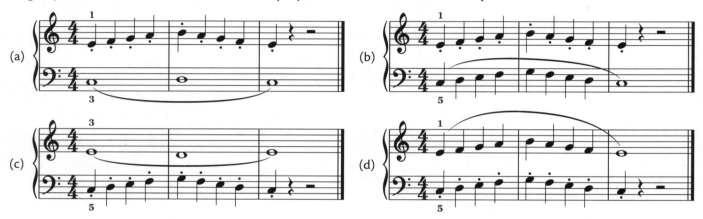

Balance of dynamics

Piano music is often written with a melody in one hand and an accompaniment in the other; these exercises will help you to **balance** the hands so that the melody comes through clearly.

The **tenuto** sign (literally meaning 'held') indicates that you should give a little extra weight to the sound by 'leaning' into the note, with full tone.

- Again, start with just the first notes, and build each exercise up gradually.

In *Romantic Story* the contrast between legato and staccato helps to bring out the flowing melody. In the first and last sections keep the left-hand staccatos light, though those in the middle section (in the right hand) can be played with a fuller tone. We've added a duet part on the CD to provide even more colour.

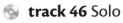 **track 46** Solo
 track 47 Duet

Romantic Story

Cornelius Gurlitt
(1820–1901)

D major scale, two octaves

The key of D major has a key signature of two sharps—F sharp and C sharp—and the fingering pattern is the same as for C and G majors. This time, try extending the scale to two octaves:

D major scale (two octaves)

Practise each hand separately, using the '**3 4 3**' **fingering pattern** to help you:

Right hand
- On the way up the thumb goes under the third finger, then under the fourth, and then under the third.
- On the way down the thumb is followed by the third finger, then the fourth, and then the third.

Left hand
- On the way up the thumb is followed by the third finger, then the fourth, and then the third.
- On the way down the thumb goes under the third finger, then under the fourth, and then under the third.

You can give your scales musical shape by making a slight crescendo as you ascend and a diminuendo as you descend. Try to avoid 'bumps' where the thumb and fingers cross.

When you are confident playing with hands separately, try them *slowly* together. It can be helpful to remember that the third fingers of each hand are always used at the same time.

Other two-octave scales

We're not suggesting you practise all these two-octave scales now, but when you begin your practice you can use them to warm up in the key of the piece you are about to play.

The '3 4 3' pattern above is also used for the following two-octave scales. The sharpened and flattened notes are indicated in brackets.

- **C major**
- **G major** (F♯)

- **A minor** (G♯)
- **D minor** (B♭ and C♯)
- **E minor** (F♯ and D♯)

F major has a different right-hand fingering pattern—'4 3 4'—although the left hand still follows the '3 4 3' pattern:

F major scale (two octaves)

Again, practise separately first, and then with hands together. A helpful hint for F major is that, apart from the highest and lowest notes, the thumbs of each hand are always used at the same time.

Here's a short piece to make use of the two-octave D major scale. Aim for clarity and evenness of rhythm in the semiquavers; the marked dynamics will help to give the music a sense of drive and direction.

vivo, **vivace** – lively

track 48 Solo

Study in D

J. B.

Moving around the keyboard

Exploring the full range of the piano requires some notational short cuts to avoid a great many leger lines. We have already encountered *8ᵛᵃ* and *8ᵛᵇ* (in book 1), but occasionally you may also come across *15ᵐᵃ* and *15ᵐᵇ*—the Italian abbreviation for 'at the fifteenth' (above or below). This means you should play the passage two octaves higher or lower than written—count the notes up and you will see!

So the highest A and the lowest A on the piano can be notated like this:

- Try this exercise to improve your piano geography, moving up by one note for each new phrase until you get to C again.
- Then work back the other way from top C down.

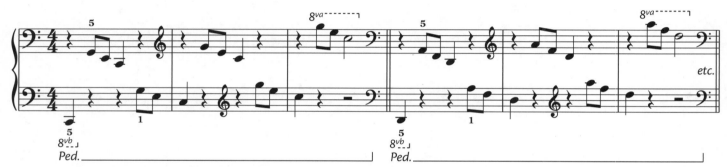

A new time signature

6/4 Six crotchet beats in the bar, grouped in two groups of three.

This can be described as a compound time signature because the crotchets are grouped in threes, making the beat a dotted minim. A **6/4** bar contains the same number of crotchets as a **3/2** bar, but in **3/2** we count three minim beats in each bar rather than two dotted minims.

track 49   track 50

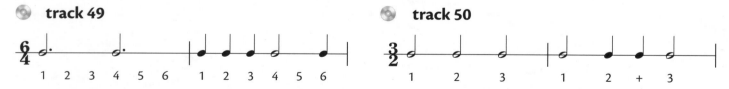

Cloudscape, on the following page, allows you to practise moving between one hand position and the next, both in the dreamy opening and the stormy middle section. It also gives you the opportunity to use the **soft pedal** (the one on the left) to produce a less rich sound. On a grand piano this pedal moves the keyboard along slightly so the hammer only hits one of the strings in the groups of three (or two), and the edge of the single strings; on an upright it usually moves the hammers a bit nearer to the strings. Always use the left foot for the soft pedal, and in the final bars hold down both the soft pedal and the sustaining pedal.

una corda – hold down the soft pedal (literally 'one string')
tre corde – take your foot off the soft pedal (literally 'three strings')

track 51 Solo

Cloudscape

A. B.

Developing your technique

This middle-page spread is a resource to come back to, and to be used over a period of time—don't try to play it through from beginning to end!

In Book 1 we suggested you develop a practice routine, beginning with a body-relaxing exercise and then moving on to warm-ups (such as those on pages 26, 30, 40, 42, and 44 of Book 1, and on pages 22, 30, 34, and 40 of this book). You will also find it very useful to warm up with scales and arpeggios in the key of the piece you're about to play. You will find that your playing develops more naturally and easily when you have warmed up, and on these two pages we suggest some further exercises that you might like to try.

Each exercise may be played:

- in the right hand or an octave lower in the left hand (the right-hand fingering is shown above the music and the left-hand fingering below it)
- with hands together
- in the alternative keys suggested, by starting on the new key-note and adding the sharps or flats for that key
- at different speeds
- *p* or *f*
- staccato or legato (in most cases).

If you find your fingers, wrists, or arms getting tense, it's time to stop, do something else, and come back later . . .

Even playing and octave leaps 1 (also play in G, D, and F majors; if hands together, play two octaves apart)

Even playing and octave leaps 2 (as above)

Steady pulse (don't start too fast! also play in G, D, and F majors)

Broken chord patterns (repeat each bar several times if you wish; also play in G, D, and F majors)

Alberti bass patterns (repeat each bar several times if you wish; also play in G, D, and F majors)

Equality of fingers (also play in G, D, and F majors)

Chords (only in C unless you're feeling brave!)

Moving around keyboard and exercising fingers (only in C)

Independence of fingers (play both lines in one hand; also play in G, D, and F majors)

Scales in octaves (play in any key you know; if playing hands together, play these and the next two exercises two octaves apart)

Rotate the wrist slightly (staccato only; play in any key)

Rotate the wrist (as above)

B flat major scale

B flat major has a key signature of two flats: B flat and E flat.

The scale fingering follows the same '3 4 3' pattern as the other scales you know, but this time you start on a different finger—the second finger in the right hand and the third in the left hand. Note also that the highest B flat in the left hand is played by the second finger rather than the third. Unfortunately, no fingers are used in both hands at the same time!

- As before, practise each hand separately, and don't worry if you find it difficult to coordinate the two hands together at this stage.

B flat major scale (two octaves)

The B flat major arpeggio will be introduced on page 50.

Less common time signatures

Theoretically you can have any number of beats in a bar and, during the last 150 years particularly, composers have experimented with the use of various 'irregular' time signatures:

$\frac{5}{4}$ Five crotchet beats in each bar. This can feel like: $\frac{2}{4} + \frac{3}{4}$ or $\frac{3}{4} + \frac{2}{4}$

$\frac{5}{8}$ Five quaver beats in each bar. This can feel like: $\frac{2}{8} + \frac{3}{8}$ or $\frac{3}{8} + \frac{2}{8}$

$\frac{7}{4}$ Seven crotchet beats in each bar. This can feel like: $\frac{4}{4} + \frac{3}{4}$ or $\frac{3}{4} + \frac{4}{4}$

Time signature changes

Sometimes the time signature changes during a piece. When this happens, the beat remains at the same speed unless otherwise indicated. If a time signature changes at the beginning of a line, it is also printed as a warning at the end of the previous line.

Time for Thought is in B flat major and has a $\frac{5}{4}$ time signature; it also introduces some time signature changes. The crotchets are always the same length, so keep the melody flowing onwards, except in the final section, where the pauses gently interrupt the melody and give you an opportunity to suggest a feeling of peaceful calm. Keeping your hands well forward will help when playing black keys with the thumb.

dolce – sweetly

track 52 Solo

Time for Thought

J. B.

'Drop and lift' slurs

You will often encounter piano music that calls on a 'drop and lift' style of playing to give lightness and character to the melodic writing.

- Practise the following examples by dropping (with arm weight) onto the first note of each slurred pair, then lifting lightly ('floating') off the second in time to prepare for the next hand position.
- Play steadily, being careful not to rush—aim for gracefulness and elegance.
- Changing fingers on the same note will help to create the 'drop and lift' effect.

- Now aim for the same effect with groups of three: drop onto the thumb and lift on the third finger.

Johann Wilhelm Hässler was a German keyboard player who wrote many sonatas and studies for the piano. He taught in Germany, London, and Moscow, where he had a big influence on the development of piano playing and composition. This *Ecossaise* (literally 'Scottish dance') comes from a collection of 'Fifty pieces for beginners', and is reminiscent of the clear-cut Classical style of Hässler's contemporaries Haydn and Mozart. Following the fingering carefully will enable you to achieve a lightness and sense of direction in the right-hand melody as you gently drop onto the first of each semiquaver group and lift on each of the staccato quavers.

giocoso – playful, merry

Ecossaise

Johann Wilhelm Hässler
(1747–1822)

Allegretto giocoso

Chromatic notes

The word **chromatic** (literally 'coloured') is used to describe any notes that are not part of the major or minor scale currently in use. Chromatic notes are often used to decorate a melody or to enrich the underlying harmony of a piece, and these effects became particularly popular during the nineteenth century—the **Romantic** period—as composers sought to present a wider variety of expression and colour in their music.

Here is a well-known example of a chromatic melody:

The **chromatic scale** moves by semitones, using the black and white keys.

- To prepare for this, practise the following exercise, hands separately, always using the third finger for the black keys and the thumb on the white keys.
- Try to 'glide' up and down the keys, playing as evenly as possible.

A chromatic scale can start on any note, and the fingering is always the same: third finger on black keys, thumb and second finger (when two white notes are next to each other) on white keys. In chromatic scales the black keys are usually notated as sharps when going up and flats when going down, although there is no hard-and-fast rule.

- Here is the chromatic scale starting on D. Practise this with hands separately to begin with.

D chromatic

Valse chromatique ('chromatic waltz') makes use of chromaticism in both the melody and the harmony. It is intended to reflect the rich musical language of composers of the Romantic period, such as Chopin. Whichever hand the melody is in, aim to achieve a 'singing' sound by using plenty of arm weight and keeping the accompaniment a little quieter.

Composers of the nineteenth century often expected the expressive style of their music to be heightened by the use of **rubato** (literally 'robbed time'), a feeling of 'give and take' in the rhythm. Don't confuse this with playing 'out of time'—the pulse and rhythm must still be felt, despite the occasional slowing down or speeding up.

molto – very, much (**molto rit**. – slow down a lot)   **,** – a slight pause

track 54 Solo

Valse chromatique

A. B.

Andante espressivo e con rubato

Harmonic building blocks

Many of the pieces you have played consist of a melody with accompaniment, and this accompaniment is usually made up of a series of chords (albeit often in a 'disguised' form, such as the Alberti bass on pages 28–9).

A succession of chords is known as **harmony** and, as with the melodic building blocks we explored in Book 1, it's possible to develop musical ideas by thinking harmonically.

Chords are often indicated by Roman numerals, and the three most frequently used are:

- the triad on the key note (**chord I**)
- the triad built on the note a fourth above the key note (**chord IV**)
- the triad built on the note a fifth above the key note (**chord V**).

The note on which the triad is based, and which gives it its name, is called the **root**.

Many tunes can be harmonized with just these three chords, known as the **primary triads**. Here they are in three different keys, laid out to make a succession of chords, or **chord progression**, starting and finishing on the key note:

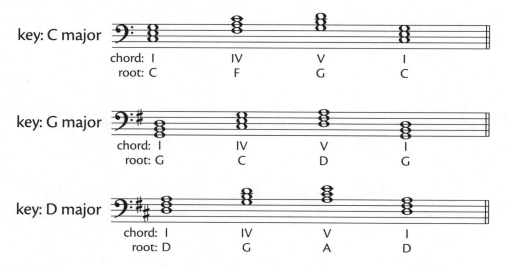

You don't have to play the chords exactly as written here; instead you could:

- play them an octave higher or lower
- play only the root (lowest note), missing out the others
- play only the lowest two notes, missing out the top one
- share out the notes between both hands (perhaps playing the lowest note in the left hand and the other two notes an octave higher in the right hand)
- break up each chord into individual notes and play them one after another in various patterns (such as Alberti bass)

and of course there are many other possibilities . . .

You might like to experiment by creating harmonic patterns from these 'building blocks'.

On 💿 **tracks 55–60** you can use chords I, IV, and V to create a backing to the musical ideas on the CD—just follow the instructions.

Adding chords to a melody

When we use these chords to harmonize a melody, the basic rule of thumb is to choose a chord that contains the melody note, although you don't need to change the chord for every note—experiment and see what sounds best. In the folk-song melodies below we've indicated where the chords change, and in some places given two options. Try the following:

- Play the melody in the right hand and the root of the chord in the left hand.
- Play the melody in the right hand and the complete triad in the left hand.
- Listen to the melody on the CD and accompany it with the chords, in any layout you choose.

track 61

Cornish Floral Dance

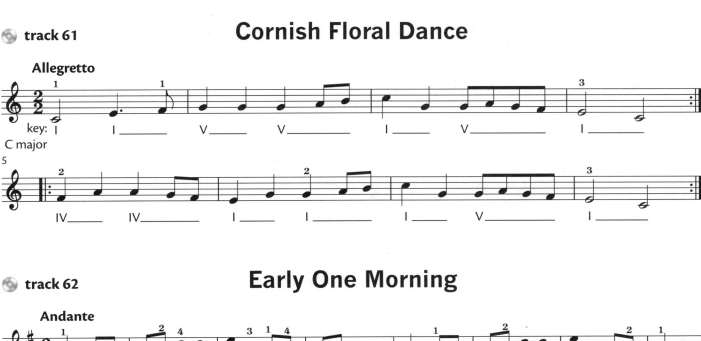

track 62

Early One Morning

track 63

I Saw Three Ships

More on pedalling

Often composers do not indicate where the sustaining pedal is to be used, or merely mark *con Ped.* ('with pedal') at the beginning of the piece. In much music, the expectation is that the pedal will be used, even though it isn't indicated.

How do we decide where to lower and raise the pedal?

- If the music is staccato, or if there are rests, it's usual to avoid using the pedal at all.
- If the music moves by step, the pedal will tend to blur the sound, so it's best to use no pedal or be very sparing in its use.
- In chordal sections, pedalling afresh on each chord will enrich the sonority.
- If the music moves in patterns such as broken chords or Alberti bass, the use of the pedal is often appropriate as it will help the notes blend together to form a complete chord.
- The most important rule is to listen and, normally, to raise the pedal as soon as the sound is starting to blur.

The practice of playing a tune (or **theme**) and then repeating it several times in a decorated or developed version goes back many hundreds of years, and most of the great composers have written **variations**, either on a pre-existing theme or on one composed specially. The theme of the *Variations on an American Spiritual* is the song 'I must walk my lonesome valley'.

We have deliberately omitted most of the sustaining pedal indications, but the piece would certainly benefit from use of the pedal. In the theme, and in variations 1 and 3, try lowering the pedal on the first beat of each bar and raising it right at the beginning of the third beat (otherwise the stepwise movement at the end of many bars will blur the harmony). By contrast, the staccato texture of the second variation would suggest no pedal.

meno – less   **mosso** – movement   **e, ed** – and
(**Poco meno mosso e misterioso** – a little slower and mysteriously)
Tempo primo (or **Tempo I**) – first tempo (back to the speed of the beginning)

🔘 **track 64** Solo

Variations on an American Spiritual

VARIATION 1

VARIATION 2
Poco meno mosso e misterioso

VARIATION 3
Tempo primo

G minor scale

G minor is the relative minor of B flat major and has a key signature of two flats: B flat and E flat. The fingering pattern for the scale is the same as for G major, but watch out for the wide gap between the sixth and seventh notes.

- Here is the scale for two octaves. As before, practise each hand separately before putting them together.

G minor scale (harmonic, two octaves)

The G minor arpeggio will be introduced on page 50.

Demisemiquavers

The **demisemiquaver** (or thirty-second-note) lasts half the length of a semiquaver; thus a quaver contains four demisemiquavers.

As with semiquavers, demisemiquavers are often grouped in fours, and they are joined by a **triple beam**.

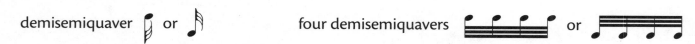

You may be pleased to hear that there are no pieces containing demisemiquavers in this book! However, they are used in the explanation of double dots below, and in the section on embellishments on page 52.

Double dots

Just as one dot after a note extends that note by half its length, two dots after a note extend it again by half the length added by the previous dot.

The double-dotted crotchet is used twice in Tchaikovsky's *Old French Song* (from his 'Album for the Young'). Counting in quavers (**1**–2–3–4–**and**) will help you to perfect this rhythm—place the notes on the '1' and the 'and'. Make sure the hands are well balanced—the right-hand part should be played with a little more arm weight than the left—and keep the staccatos very light in bars 9–12. Allow for the *pp* repeat of the first section by not beginning too quietly.

track 65 Solo

Old French Song

Pyotr Il'yich Tchaikovsky
(1840–93)

Arpeggios, two octaves

As with scales, we can now extend arpeggios to two octaves.

Here is the **C major** arpeggio for each hand:

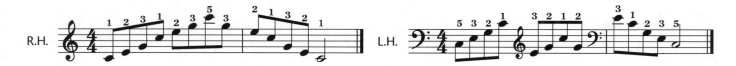

The thumbs and the third fingers have a long way to travel, and the following exercise will help you make a smooth join.

- Swing the hand quickly round, pivoting with the wrist and not the elbow.
- Always try to keep your fingers, hands, and arms relaxed.

Exactly the same fingering pattern is used with all but one of the other keys you already know. The sharpened and flattened notes are indicated in brackets.

- **G major**
- **F major**
- **D major** (F♯)

- **A minor**
- **D minor**
- **E minor**
- **G minor** (B♭)

B flat major starts on a black note, so the fingering is different:

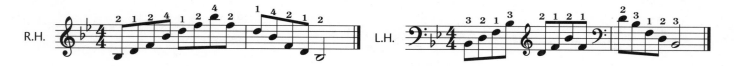

As with the two-octave scales, we're not suggesting that you practise all these arpeggios at once. Use them when you begin your practice to warm up in the key of the piece you are about to play.

Aim to give each arpeggio a musical shape, with a slight crescendo in the first bar and a diminuendo in the second, but for the moment only practise them with hands separately.

More playing at sight

Here are some short pieces to play at sight.

Remind yourself of the hints on page 21, and remember to always keep the music moving on.

Before playing:

- check the time and key signatures
- think through (or tap) the rhythm
- look out for any changes of hand position
- play the dynamics to add the 'finishing touch'.

alla – in the style of   **alla marcia** – in the style of a march   **grave** – slow and solemn

Miniature March

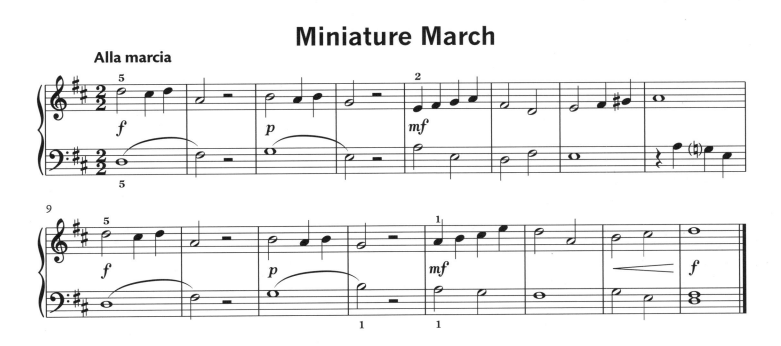

Melancholy Meditation

Grace notes and ornaments

Throughout the history of keyboard music composers and performers have used decorations (or **embellishments**) to enhance the character of the music, just as jazz and folk players do today. In most piano music of the classical tradition, players are only expected to embellish the music where indicated, and a number of signs are used for this purpose. Some of these signs had slightly different meanings in different periods of musical history, and there have been entire books written on this subject. Here we give just a brief summary of the main embellishments that you may come across, all of which are played on 🔘 **track 66**

Grace notes are printed smaller than normal notes and on the page appear to take up no time because the larger notes 'add up' to a complete bar without them. In fact, they do take some time out of the notes they precede, but they shouldn't interfere with the flow of the music or the regularity of the pulse. There are two main types of grace note:

- **Appoggiatura** (leaning note) – takes half the time of the note it precedes, and therefore reduces the main note to half its length.

(with no line through the stem)

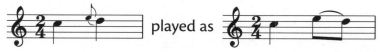

- **Acciaccatura** (crushed note) – should be played as quickly as possible, reducing the length of the main note slightly as a result. Sometimes, according to taste, it is played slightly before the beat.

(with a little line through the stem)

Ornaments are indicated by a symbol above the note and, like grace notes, should not interfere with the musical flow or the pulse. A sharp or flat may be added above or below the symbol (as applicable) for any ornament, as in the example of the lower mordent below. The most common examples are:

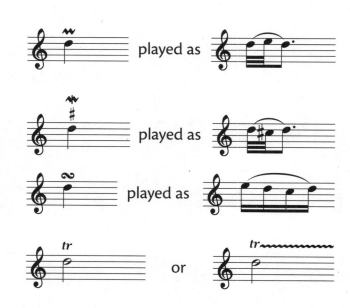

- **Mordent** (or **upper mordent**) – play the written note, then the note above, and then the written note again. The first two notes should be played as quickly as possible, and the final note should take up the remaining time.
- **Lower mordent** – play the written note, then the note below, and then the written note again.
- **Turn** – play the note above the written note, then the written note, then the note below, and then the written note again. The notes are usually (but not always) of equal length.
- **Trill** – alternate the written note with the note above as fast as you can and as many times as will fit into the allocated time.

The secret of playing embellishments is to make them sound natural, and not to let them interrupt the flow of the music. If you find it hard to keep the music moving in time, it's better to miss them out!

Nann's Maske is an anonymous dance from a seventeenth-century collection of harpsichord pieces called 'Elizabeth Rogers' Virginal Book' (a virginal is a small harpsichord). As harpsichords could not achieve dynamic contrast, ornaments were frequently used to give colour to the musical line. In the original there is an ornament on every beat, which would have been easier to play on the virginal, with its light touch, than on the present day piano. We have indicated just a few embellishments, but we suggest you learn the piece without them first so the rhythm is clear in your mind. We have also added suggestions for dynamics and phrasing.

Larghetto – quite slow, but not as slow as **Largo**

 **track 67** Solo

Nann's Maske

Larghetto

Anon. (17th century)

New compound time signatures

Here are two new compound time signatures. Remember that each dotted crotchet beat is divisible by three.

9/8 Nine quavers in each bar, grouped in threes, giving three dotted crotchet beats per bar.

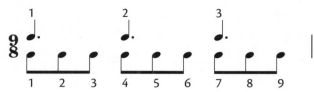

12/8 Twelve quavers in each bar, grouped in threes, giving four dotted crotchet beats per bar.

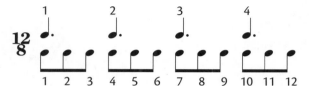

The Shamrock, in **9/8**, is based on a traditional fiddle tune and is full of the energy of a Celtic folk dance. Count three dotted crotchet beats in the bar, keeping the melody going steadily and evenly.

🔘 **track 68** Solo

The Shamrock

Trad.

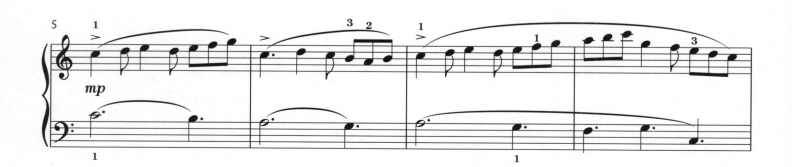

Modes

The word **mode** (or modal scale) is often used to describe a scale that is not either major or minor. This can include scales using only white notes but not starting on C, and the **pentatonic** (or five-note) scale using only the black notes. You have already encountered some of these modes in Book 1: *Autumn* (page 28) uses the white-note mode starting on D, and *Mystical Memories* (page 47) uses the pentatonic scale. The use of these modes goes back many centuries.

Since the beginning of the twentieth century many composers have sought to achieve a different harmonic character in their music by calling on an even wider range of modes. Two favoured by twentieth-century composers are:

- the **whole-tone** scale, in which all the notes are a tone apart (used by Debussy); and
- the **octatonic** (eight-note) scale, which alternates tones and semitones (used by Stravinsky and Messiaen).

Whole-tone scale

Octatonic scale

You might like to try experimenting with these modal scales, perhaps by using them as a melodic basis for the rhythms you explored earlier in the book. They can sound rich and sonorous when played with the sustaining pedal down.

Modal Melody uses the octatonic scale to create rich and unusual harmonies. The staccato dots with slurs above or below them (bars 5–6) indicate **semi-staccatos**—the notes should be slightly separated but not as short as staccatos. In the second section, the linked quaver groups (across the two staves) indicate that the melody should flow smoothly between the hands.

Arpeggio, on the next page, achieves its harmonic originality by juxtaposing chords or note patterns in unexpected key relationships. Although he has written larger works, Howard Skempton is particularly known for his 'miniatures' for various instruments, which often approach simple musical ideas in an unusual and surprising way. Skempton comments that this piece 'requires a light touch. The sounds should "ring", as suggested by the open ties. Use of the right pedal as indicated ensures the necessary fullness of harmony'. The tempo indication is a **metronome marking** (or **M.M.**, which actually stands for 'Maelzel's Metronome') of approximately (*c.*) 56 crotchet beats per minute. This pulse can be obtained from an electronic or clockwork metronome.

🎵 **track 69** Solo

Modal Melody

A. B.

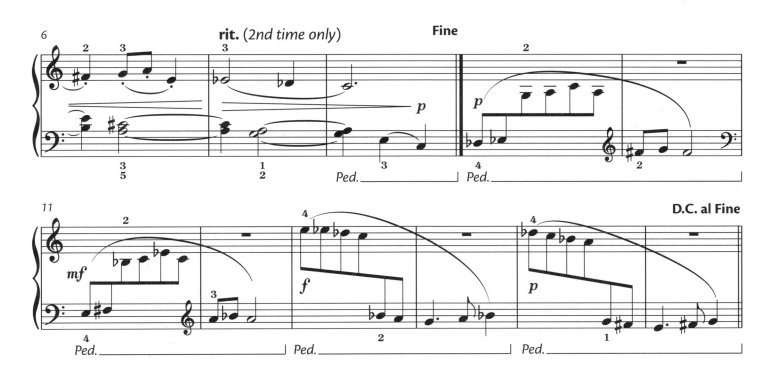

for Thalia Myers

Arpeggio

track 70 Solo

Howard Skempton
(b. 1947)

E flat major and C minor scales and arpeggios

These two new keys share the same three-flat key signature, as C minor is the relative minor of E flat major.

E flat major scale (two octaves)

E flat major arpeggio (two octaves)

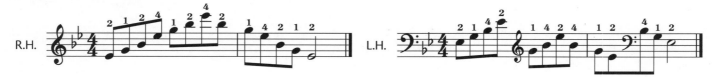

The fingering patterns for the C minor scale and arpeggio are the same as for C major.

C minor scale (harmonic, two octaves)

C minor arpeggio (two octaves)

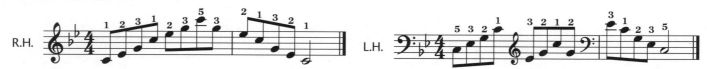

There is a piece in C minor to play on page 66.

This *Andante in E flat* is taken from Mozart's 'London Notebook', written, at the age of eight, while he was on tour in London with his father and sister. While he was there, Mozart took the opportunity to study with J. C. Bach, one of J. S. Bach's sons, who had successfully settled in England as a composer of music in the newly popular 'classical' style. The original is incomplete, so we've repeated some of the earlier bars to make a short piece, and added dynamics and phrase marks. The 'drop and lift' slurs will help to shape the melodic line.

In bar 4 the appoggiatura and the quaver that follows should be played as two equal semiquavers of E flat and D.

track 71 Solo

Andante in E flat

W. A. Mozart
(1756–91)

A major scale and arpeggio

The key of A major has a key signature of three sharps, and the scale and arpeggio share the same fingering patterns as C major.

A major scale (two octaves)

A major arpeggio (two octaves)

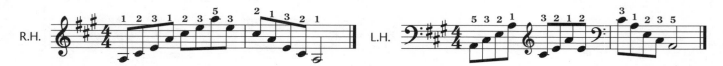

Spread chords

A vertical wavy line before a chord means that the notes should be **spread** (or arpeggiated), i.e. played in succession as quickly as possible, starting with the lowest and finishing with the highest. The wavy line can be on a single stave, or it can cover both staves, in which case the right hand doesn't start to play until all the left-hand notes have been sounded.

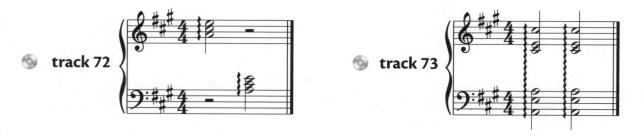

track 72   track 73

The song 'Simple Gifts' was written by a member of the American Shaker community in 1848. The words begin "Tis the gift to be simple, 'tis the gift to be free' and later speak of the 'valley of love and delight, where true simplicity is gained'. Aim to capture a feeling of both strength and gentleness in this arrangement.

semplice – simply

track 74 Solo

Simple Gifts

American Shaker melody

Two nineteenth-century pieces

Here are two arrangements of popular pieces from the Romantic period to add to your repertoire: Schubert's melodious Entr'acte No. 3 from the ballet *Rosamunde* (repeats optional) and Smetana's *Vltava*—a portrait of the River Danube near its source high in the hills. Note that the changes in tempo and the pause in *Vltava* are omitted in 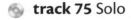 **track 77** (duet track).

track 75 Solo

Entr'acte No. 3
from *Rosamunde*

Franz Schubert
(1797–1828)

track 76 Solo
track 77 Duet

Vltava

from *Má vlast*

Bedřich Smetana
(1824–84)

Allegretto cantabile

Wistful is a **jazz waltz**, an expressive style of piece that was developed in the twentieth century. The quavers may be played straight (even) or swung—though preferably not both at the same time! When playing in swing, remember that the first quaver in each group is always longer than the second. Despite the lazy feel to the quavers, the basic pulse should be absolutely steady. You might like to experiment with a little embellishment too, as on the solo swing version on the CD. The duet track provides a rhythmic backing of crotchets, designed to help you feel the beat when playing in swing.

🔘 **track 78** Solo (straight)
🔘 **track 79** Solo (swing)
🔘 **track 80** Duet (swing)

Wistful

A. B.

Improvising using swing rhythms

On 🔘 **tracks 81–6** you'll find some call and response and improvisation exercises. Just follow the instructions on the CD.

More musical signs and Italian terms

Coda – 'tail' or ending section

D.S. al Coda (or **Dal Segno al Coda**) – go back to 𝄋, then jump from ⊕ to the **CODA**
(**da** or **dal** – from; **a** or **al** – to)

𝑠𝑓 (*sforzando*) – heavily accented

accent – usually more powerful than

staccatissimo – a very short staccato

One of a family of German musicians, Johann Friedrich Franz Burgmüller settled in Paris and became a popular pianist and composer. This dramatic *Ballade*, with its contrasts of mood, chromatic harmony, and wide dynamic range, is characteristic of much early nineteenth-century music, and it brings together many of the techniques we have been studying in this book.

The piece begins in the key of C minor (see page 58 for the scale and arpeggio), but later modulates to C major—note the natural signs cancelling the flats of the key signature at the beginning of bar 31—and returns to C minor in bar 57. It uses all the signs described at the bottom of page 65.

col, con – with   **con brio** – with vigour

track 87 Solo

Ballade
Op. 100 No. 15

J. F. F. Burgmüller
(1806–74)

Allegro con brio

And finally a celebratory duet that you can play with a friend (or with the CD).

In duets, the two parts are often printed on facing pages, as here, with the lower part (**secondo**) printed on the left-hand page and the upper part (**primo**) on the right-hand page. When playing duets, always listen carefully to the balance to ensure that the melody (whether in primo or secondo) can be heard over the accompaniment. The secondo player usually takes care of the pedalling.

In this arrangement of the traditional Mexican song *La cucuracha* ('The cockroach') you both get a chance to play the main tune. Count carefully through the rests and long notes to ensure that you stay together.

Best wishes for your future piano playing!

JANET AND ALAN BULLARD

SECONDO

track **88** Full performance (both parts)

track **89** Secondo part only

La cucuracha

Trad. Mexican

PRIMO

track 90 Primo part only

La cucuracha

Trad. Mexican

Index

Those musical terms in this book that are not found here will be found in Book 1.

Visual index

Sign	Page	Sign	Page
♪ 𝅘𝅥 ♫♫ ♫	6	𝅗𝅥 𝅝	30
♪ ♩.	18	⌐⌐ 𝅘𝅥 𝅘𝅥	56
3 ♩♩♩ ♪♩♩ 3	20	sf ♩ ♩ ♩ ♩	65
♪ 𝅘𝅥 ♬♬ ♬	48	Ped. ✿	18
𝅗𝅥.. 𝅗𝅥.. ♩.	48	,	42
2/2 ¢ 3/2 3/8	14	𝄋 ⊕	65
6/4	34	15ᵐᵃ----- 15ᵐᵇ-----	34
5/4 5/8 7/4	38	♩ = c.56	56
9/8 12/8	54	♪ ♪ ♪♪ ♪♪ ∞ tr~~~~	52
		⌇	60

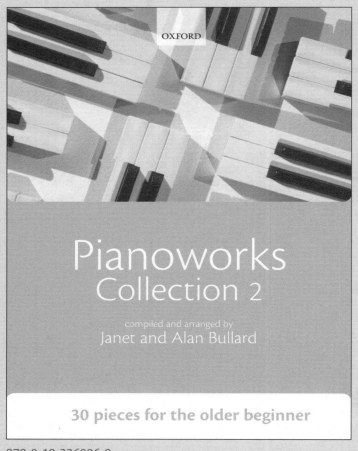

OXFORD

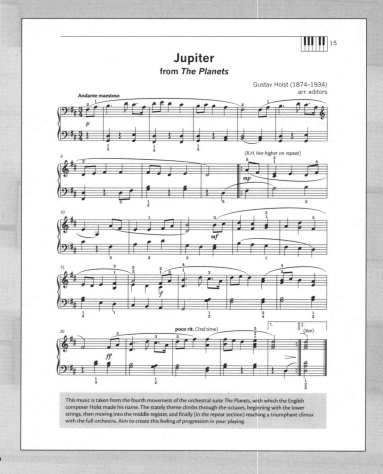

978-0-19-336006-8

Contents

Henry VIII: *Pastime with good company* •
Verdi: *La donna e mobile* • Purcell: *Air* •
Joplin: *Peacherine Rag* • Schubert:
Heidenröslein • Sullivan: *Poor wandering one*
• Steibelt: *Adagio* • J. Bullard: *Whatever* •
Trad.: *The water is wide* • Sousa: *Liberty Bell* •
Tchaikovsky: *Danse arabe* • Holst: *Jupiter* •
Couperin: *Le petit-rien* • Handel: *He shall
feed his flock* • Haydn: *Allegro* • A. Bullard:
On the edge • J. S. Bach: *Prelude* • Desmond:
Take Five • Beethoven: *Theme from
Symphony No. 6* • Reinecke: *Prelude* •
Brahms: *Sonntag* • Mozart: *Là ci darem la
mano* • Nichols: *We've only just begun* •
Dowland: *Flow, my tears* • Alwyn: *The Sea is
Angry* • Clementi: *Sonatina in C* • Trad.:
Scarborough Fair • Trad.: *Steal Away*

❖ Perfect companion to *Pianoworks Book 2*
❖ 30 pieces for beginner pianists
❖ Classical and Romantic favourites,
   popular songs and show tunes, easy
   contemporary pieces, traditional
   melodies, and new works by the authors
❖ Short notes giving tips on style and
   technique, and informative background
   information on the pieces.

www.oup.com/uk/music

For the older beginner